Table of Contents

Introduction

Pasta makes a staple in the diet of an average American, and an average American consumes almost 20 pounds pasta on an annual basis. Pasta offers energy and essential nutrients in the form of vitamins, minerals, and fiber. Pasta is healthy for the following benefits:

Cholesterol-free and Low Sodium

Pasta is cholesterol-free and low in sodium; therefore, it is healthy for everyone. One cup of pasta is a good source of essential nutrients, such as B-vitamins and iron. Whole wheat pasta offers 25 percent fiber.

Sustained Energy

Pasta supplies crucial fuel and glucose to your muscles and brain. It provides complex carbohydrates to your body that provides a slow discharge of energy. Unlike ordinary sugars, pasta sustains energy in your body instead of fleeing.

Folic Acid

Pasta is enriched with folic acid that is essential for pregnant women. Pasta contains essential vitamins, and one serving of Pasta provides 100 micrograms folic acid to your body.

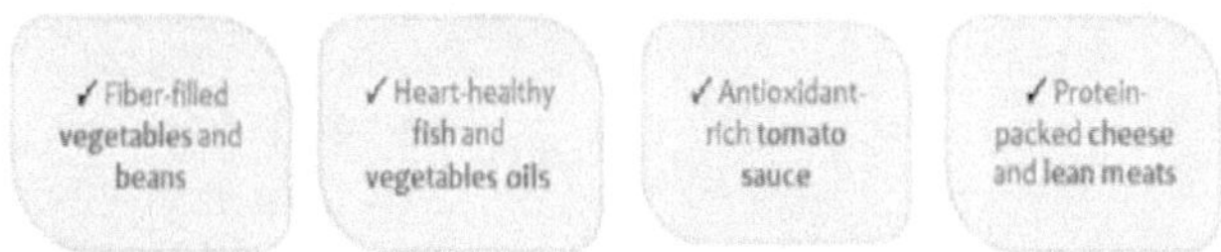

Whole-wheat pasta offers a considerable amount of dietary fiber to fight with chronic diseases, such as type-2 diabetes and obesity. Whole-wheat and white pasta serve as a great source of selenium and mineral that activates antioxidant enzymes for the protection of your body cells. Pasta contains manganese that is helpful to metabolize carbohydrates and regulate blood sugar. Whole-wheat pasta can increase 1.9 milligrams manganese in your body. White pasta provides a good amount of Vitamin B-9 and folate to your body. Whole-wheat pasta contains almost 113 micrograms zeaxanthin and lutein.

You can make pasta healthy with the help of lean protein, healthy fats, and vegetables. You can use olive oil and coconut oil along with chopped olives (Kalamata) and lemon juice to make pasta salad. In this book, you will learn 25 methods to cook delicious pasta. You can combine pasta with tomato sauce, meat, vegetables, pepper and even berries to enhance its taste. Follow the recipes given in this book:

Chapter 1 – Pasta and Noodle Recipes

There are a few methods to prepare pasta and noodles with some particular taste and flavors. Enjoy these recipes:

Recipe 01: Homemade Pasta

Cooking Time: 15 minutes

Servings: 3

Ingredients:

- Beaten egg: 1
- All-purpose flour: 1 cup
- Water: 2 tablespoons
- Salt: ½ teaspoon

Directions:

Take a medium bowl and combine salt and flour. Make a hole in the flour and add lightly whisked egg and mix them well. You have to make a firm dough. You can add 1 – 2 tablespoons water to manage the firmness of your dough.

Sprinkle light flour on a surface and knead the dough on this surface for almost 3 – 4 minutes. Use a pasta machine or manually roll dough to get desired thickness. Use knife or machine to cut the long strips of your preferred width.

Recipe 02: Summer Squash Pasta

Cooking Time: 25 minutes

Servings: 4

Ingredients:

- kosher salt
- Spaghetti: 1/2 lb.
- Yellow zucchini: 1 lb.
- Pesto: 10 oz.
- Grated Parmesan: 1/4 cup
- Cherry tomatoes (halved): 1 cup
- Olive oil: As per need
- Black pepper (ground)

Directions:

Take a pot and fill it with water and salt. Let the water boil and cook pasta according to the instructions given on the package. Meanwhile, you have to trim the one end of zucchini and pop in the flat end into one spiralizer. Zoodles can be long, but you can cut them into 7 inches' lengths. Put noodles in one colander and sprinkle salt (1 tablespoon) on the zoodles. Mix them and keep aside.

Mix drained Zoodles in the spaghetti in the last minutes of cooking. Drain noodles and put them back in the stock pot. Mix pesto sauce in noodles and transfer to one large platter and top with tomatoes and parmesan. Sprinkle black pepper and serve.

Recipe 03: Mexican Pasta

Cooking Time: 30 minutes

Servings: 4

Ingredients:

- Spaghetti: 12 oz.
  - Olive oil: 1 tablespoon
- Chicken (cubed): 1 lb.
- Onion (sliced): 1 large
- Bell peppers (sliced): 2
- Chili powder: 1 tablespoon
- Cumin: 1 tablespoon
- Dried oregano: 2 teaspoons
- Fire-roasted tomatoes: 15-oz.
- Chicken broth (low-sodium): ½ cup
- Half & half: ¾ cup
- Shredded Cheddar: ½ cup
- Pepper jack (shredded): ½ cup
- Fresh cilantro: serving time

Directions:

Take a pot of salted water and let it boil, cook spaghetti according to the instructions given on the package. Drain and set aside.

Take a large cooking pan on medium heat and heat oil. Add chicken and cook for almost 6 minutes. Sprinkle pepper and salt and mix them well. Add pepper and onion and cook for approximately 4 minutes or more to tender. Add cumin, oregano and chili powder and stir them well to coat all ingredients.

Add tomatoes to this mixture and stir this mixture well. Add half-and-half and chicken broth and stir. Add spaghetti (cooked) to your cooking pan and toss to coat all ingredients. Add cheese and cream in this mixture and garnish with chopped cilantro. Serve hot.

Recipe 04: Angel-Hair Primavera

Cooking Time: 45 minutes

Servings: 4

Ingredients:

- Angel hair: 12 oz.
- Broccoli florets: 2 cups
- kosher salt
- Cherry tomatoes (red and yellow): 1 pt.
- Baby-bella mushrooms: 1 8-oz.
- Artichoke hearts (drained & chopped): 15-oz.
- Garlic powder: 2 teaspoons
- Black pepper: ground
- Grated Parmesan: 3/4 cup + for garnishing
- Chopped basil

Directions:

Preheat an oven to almost 400 degrees F. Take a large pot with salt and water, let it boil and cook pasta as per instructions that are given on the package. Drain and reserve one cup pasta water. Return this water to the pot and keep it aside.

Take a baking sheet and add a mixture of artichoke hearts, tomatoes, toss broccoli, olive oil, garlic powder, mushrooms, pepper, and salt. Roast it for almost 15 to 20 minutes.

Add vegetables to the pot with pasta water and cook on low heat. Mix well to create a thick sauce. You can add extra pasta water as per your needs.

Garnish with basil and parmesan and serve hot.

Recipe 05: Spaghetti with Spinach and Tomato

Cooking Time: 20 to 30 minutes

Servings: 4

Ingredients:

- Spaghetti: 12 oz.
- Olive oil: 1 tablespoon
- Chopped Garlic: 2 cloves
- Italian sausage (cooked) links (sliced): 3/4 lb.
- Baby Spinach: 3 cups
- Sun-dried tomatoes (chopped): ½ cup

- Chicken broth (low-sodium): ¾ cup
- Heavy cream: ¾ cup
- kosher salt
- Black pepper as per taste
- Grated Parmesan: Garnishing

Directions:

Take one large pot with salt and water. Let this water boil and cook spaghetti as per instructions given on the package.

Take a large pot and put it on medium heat. Now, heat oil and cook garlic to get fragrance for one minute. Add spinach, dried tomatoes and sausage and cook them until sausage turns brown and spinach is completely cooked. It will take almost 3 – 5 minutes. Add heavy cream and chicken broth to let them simmer. Let the sauce turn creamy and add spaghetti to this pan. Toss spaghetti with sauce and sprinkle pepper and salt. Garnish with cilantro and parmesan and serve hot.

Chapter 2 – Summer Pasta Recipes

If you want something delicious and healthy in the summer season, there are a few recipes for you:

Recipe 06: Chicken Pasta Salad

Cooking Time: 1 hour

Servings: 3 to 4

Ingredients:

- 6oz whole wheat pasta
- 2 tomatoes, chopped
- 1 yellow bell sliced pepper
- 1 cup chopped cauliflower
- Cooked Chicken (cubed): 1 cup
- 1 3-4oz sliced olives
- 1 small chopped yellow onion
- 1/2 cup butter
- 1 tablespoon sugar

- 2 tablespoons vinegar
- Salt & pepper as per taste

Instructions:

In the first step, take salted boiling water and cook pasta as per the instructions given on the packet. It will be good to add cauliflower in water before removing pasta from heat. Let it cook for almost 45 minutes and throw the water and rinse the Pasta and cauliflower with cold water.

In a large bowl, add pasta, onions, bell pepper, cauliflower, chicken and tomato. Mix them well and then add black olives, sugar, vinegar, salt, and pepper. Mix all the ingredients well and keep in a refrigerator before serving time.

Recipe 07: Vegetable Summer Pasta

Cooking Time: 1 hour

Servings: 04

Ingredients:

- 6oz pasta
- 2 medium tomatoes, chopped
- 1 small chopped onion
- Chopped cabbage: 1 cup
- 4oz sliced olives
- 1/4 cup fat-free mayonnaise

- 1 tablespoon brown sugar

- 2 tablespoons vinegar

- Salt & pepper as per taste

Directions:

In the first step, cook pasta as per the instructions that are given on the packet. It will be good to add cabbage in water before removing the pasta from heat. Let it cook for 45 minutes and then throw the water and rinse the Pasta and Broccoli with cold water.

In a large bowl, add pasta, onions, cabbage, and tomato. Mix them well and then add black olives, sugar, vinegar, salt, and pepper. Mix all the ingredients well and keep in a refrigerator before serving them.

Recipe 08: Pasta Salad with Egg

Cooking Time: 25 minutes

Servings: 4

Ingredients:

- Eggs: 8
- Paprika: 1 teaspoon

- Bacon (chopped strips): ½ cup
- Minced Red onion: ½
- Mayonnaise: 1 tablespoon
- Pasta: 7 oz
- Pepper and salt
- Dijon Mustard: 2 tablespoons
- Dill weed: 1 tablespoon

Directions:

Boil eggs and peel them to chop into small pieces. Keep them aside.

Cook pasta as per instructions given on the package and keep it aside.

Take a large bowl and mix mustard, mayonnaise, egg, dill, onion, salt, pepper, bacon, pasta and paprika. Mash all these ingredients well with a wooden spoon or fork. Serve with your favorite sauce.

Recipe 09: Beef Pasta

Cooking Time: 1 hour

Servings: 3 to 4

Ingredients:

- 6oz whole wheat pasta

- 2 tomatoes, chopped

- 1 yellow bell sliced pepper

- 1 cup chopped cauliflower

- Cooked beef (cubed): 1 cup

- 1 3-4oz sliced olives

- 1 small chopped yellow onion

- 1/2 cup butter

- 1 tablespoon sugar

- 2 tablespoons vinegar

- Salt & pepper as per taste

Instructions:

In the first step, take salted boiling water and cook pasta as per the instructions given on the packet. It will be good to add cauliflower in water before removing pasta from heat. Let it cook for almost 45 minutes and throw the water and rinse the Pasta and cauliflower with cold water.

In a large bowl, add pasta, onions, bell pepper, cauliflower, beef and tomato. Mix them well and then add black olives, sugar, vinegar, salt, and pepper. Mix all the ingredients well and keep in a refrigerator before serving time.

Recipe 10: Fish Pasta
Cooking Time: 30 minutes

Servings: 4

Ingredients:

- Spaghetti: 12 oz.
- Olive oil: 1 tablespoon
- Cooked Fish (cubed): 1 lb.
- Onion (sliced): 1 large
- Cauliflower: 2
- Chili powder: 1 tablespoon
- Cumin: 1 tablespoon
- Dried oregano: 2 teaspoons
- Fire-roasted tomatoes: 15-oz.
- Chicken broth (low-sodium): ½ cup
- Half & half: ¾ cup
- Shredded Cheddar: ½ cup
- Pepper jack (shredded): ½ cup
- Fresh cilantro: serving time

Directions:

Take a pot of salted water and let it boil, cook spaghetti according to the instructions given on the package. Drain and set aside.

Take a large cooking pan on medium heat and heat oil. Add fish and cook for almost 6 minutes. Sprinkle pepper and salt and mix them well. Add pepper and onion and cook for approximately 4 minutes or more to tender. Add cumin, oregano and chili powder and stir them well to coat all ingredients.

Add tomatoes to this mixture and stir this mixture well. Add half-and-half and chicken broth and stir. Add spaghetti (cooked) to your cooking pan and toss to coat all ingredients. Add cheese and cream in this mixture and garnish with chopped cilantro. Serve hot.

Chapter 3 – Pasta Salad Recipes

If you want pasta salad, you can get the advantage of these recipes. There are a few essential recipes for your help:

Recipe 11: Pasta Salad with Chicken and Vegetables

If you want something delicious and healthy in the summer season, there are a few recipes for you:

Total Cooking Time: 15 to 30 minutes

Servings: 2 to 3

Ingredients:

- 4-ounce cooked chicken meat
- 2 chopped tomatoes
- Cabbage: 1 cup
- 10-ounce romaine salad
- 1/4 cup fresh cheese
- Pasta: 6 oz.

Directions:

Cook pasta according to the instructions given on the package.

Grill chicken on a griller on medium heat. Grill chicken meat for almost 2 to 3 minutes and turn its sides to let it done properly. Now remove from grill, let it cool and make cubes.

Now, gently mix cabbage, chicken cubes tomato and lettuce in a large bowl. Mix pasta and equally divide salad among four bowls and sprinkle 1 tablespoon of cheese on every serving.

Recipe 12: Cabbage Soup Pasta

Cooking Time: 40 minutes

Servings: 6

Ingredients:

- 3 cloves garlic
- 1 onion
- 8oz. pasta
- 2 to 3 carrots
- 1.5 cups cabbage
- 1.5 cups cut beans
- Handful spinach
- Salt to taste
- 1.5 cups peas
- 8 cups vegetable broth
- 1.5 cups corn

- 15 oz. diced tomatoes
- Rice and herbs

Directions:

Cook pasta as per instructions given on the package and keep aside.

Chop all vegetables and cook in the stockpot on the medium heat. Cook for 5 to 7 minutes and add garlic to cook for 30 seconds. Now add the broth and cook all vegetables except spinach. Reduce heat and cook for 20 to 30 minutes to make the vegetables soft. Add pasta and mix these ingredients well. Now mix the spinach and salt as per taste. Serve hot.

Recipe 13: Pasta and Spinach

Cooking Time: 30 minutes

Servings: 4

Ingredients

- 1-pound grilled chicken, trimmed
- 3 nectarines, halved
- 1/4 cup balsamic vinaigrette, light
- 6-ounce baby spinach, fresh
- Pasta: 8oz.
- 1/4 cup feta cheese
- Black Pepper, ground (Optional)

Directions:

Prepare a grill.

Cut chicken to make small strips with a sharp knife and grill on a grill rack greased with cooking spray. You can grill each side for five minutes at 160° (check thermometer). It is time to grill nectarines for 4 to 5 minutes on every side and remove both chicken and nectarine from the grill. Leave it for 10 minutes.

Cook pasta as per instructions given on the package and keep it aside.

Use a sharp knife to divide nectarine into slices and make thin slices of chicken. Mix vinaigrette and spinach in a large bowl. Add pasta and mix it gently to coat everything. It is time to divide spinach mixture equally in 6 plates. Now top every plate equally with nectarine and chicken slices. Sprinkle cheese and pepper as per your taste.

Recipe 14: Pasta Salad with Bacon

Cooking Time: 30 to 45 Minutes

Serving: 4

Ingredients:

- 1/4 teaspoon black pepper, ground
- Pasta: 8 ounces
- 1/4 teaspoon salt
- 1/4 cup fresh onion, minced
- 6-ounce chicken breast without skin
- 2 bacon, slices

- 3/4 cup apple cider, without sugar

- 1/2 cups chicken broth, without salt and fat

Directions:

Cook pasta as per instructions given on the package.

Take a chicken breast and keep between 2 durable plastic sheets to make a wrap. The meat should be ½ inch thick and you can use a rolling pin to make it flat. Sprinkle salt and pepper on chicken.

Now, take a large cooking pan to cook bacon on medium heat to make it crisp. Remove this bacon from a cooking pan and add chicken in the similar pan. Cook every side for six minutes or until it is completely done. Remove this chicken from the pan and keep it warm.

Now add onion in the cooking pan and cook for two minutes, stir the spoon frequently and add broth and cider. Let it boil and scrape the pan to drop brown bits in the soup. Cook the both mixtures to reduce the broth to ½ cup. It may take five minutes. It is time to mix cooked bacon and pasta and serve with sauce on chicken.

Recipe 15: Mexican Pasta Salad

Cooking Time: 30 minutes

Servings: 4

Ingredients:

- Spaghetti: 12 oz.
  - Olive oil: 1 tablespoon
- Beef (cubed): 1 lb.
- Onion (sliced): 1 large
- Chili powder: 1 tablespoon
- Cumin: 1 tablespoon
- Dried oregano: 2 teaspoons
- Tomato Paste: 15-oz.
- Beef broth (low-sodium): ½ cup
- Half & half: ¾ cup
- Shredded Cheese: ½ cup
- Pepper jack (shredded): ½ cup
- Fresh cilantro: serving time

Directions:

Take a pot of salted water and let it boil, cook spaghetti according to the instructions given on the package. Drain and set aside.

Take a large cooking pan on medium heat and heat oil. Add beef and cook for almost 6 minutes. Sprinkle pepper and salt and mix them well. Add onion and cook for approximately 4 minutes or more to tender. Add cumin, oregano and chili powder and stir them well to coat all ingredients.

Add tomatoes paste to this mixture and stir this mixture well. Add half-and-half and broth and stir. Add spaghetti (cooked) to your cooking pan and toss to coat all ingredients. Add cheese and cream in this mixture and garnish with chopped cilantro. Serve hot.

Chapter 4 – Pasta and Meat Recipes

You can try these meat and pasta recipes to improve your health. These are really delicious for everyone!

Recipe 16: Pasta and Sausage

Cooking Time: 30 minutes

Servings: 4

Ingredients:

- 3 tablespoons olive oil
- 8 eggs
- 12 oz crumbled Italian sausage
- ½ chopped onion
- 1 cup cheese (ricotta)
- 2 cups chopped spinach
- ½ teaspoon sea salt
- Pasta: 8 ounce

- 1 cup chopped mushrooms

- ¼ cup chopped cheese (Parmesan)

Directions:

Cook pasta as per instructions given on the package.

Prepare an oven at 350º F. Whisk eggs in a medium bowl and mix olive oil in the mixture. Keep it aside.

Take an oven proof pan and cook onion and sausage in a medium heat with one tablespoon olive oil. Let the onions turn light brown and then add pepper and salt. Now add spinach and cover it after mixing it. After 2 minutes, add ricotta, salt, and mushrooms. It is time to pour the eggs and pasta, and mix this blend well. Now cover it on a medium heat for 3 minutes.

Now sprinkle parmesan cheese on the top and keep this pan in over for almost 20 minutes. After removing from oven, let it cool for five minutes and then release it from the edges with a spatula. Divide it into slices before serving.

Recipe 17: Brussels Sprouts, Pasta and Chicken

Cooking Time: 30 minutes

Servings: 4

Ingredients:

- 2 cloves crushed garlic
- 2 tablespoons coconut oil
- 1 chopped onion
- 1 pound Brussels sprouts, bisected
- 1 sweet potato, cubed
- ¼ cup Parmesan cheese (grated)
- Cooked Pasta: 8 oz.
- 4 ounces chopped mushrooms
- 12 oz ham, (precooked and cubed)
- 1 teaspoon sea salt
- 4 eggs

Directions:

Cook pasta as per instructions given on the package.

Prepare an oven in advance at 350°F.

Take a large skillet and cook garlic and onion with oil on a medium heat for 2 minutes. Now add Brussels, potato, mushrooms and salt. Mix it well and then cover for 7 to 8 minutes. You can mix it occasionally. Now mix ham and pasta, and use 4 spoons to make depressions in the mixture. Now crack an egg into each depression and sprinkle cheese on the top.

Transfer the pan in oven and bake for 10 minutes.

Recipe 18: Tasty Chicken Balls with Pasta

Cooking Time: 1 hour 10 minutes

Servings: 5

Ingredients:

- ¾ cup hot sauce
- ½ cup butter, melted
- 1 teaspoon sea salt
- 2 tablespoons vinegar
- 1 cup sour cream
- Blue Cheese (Dressing)
- 1 cup mayonnaise
- Pasta: 8 oz.
- ½ teaspoon sea salt
- 3 pounds chicken mince
- 1 cup crushed cheese
- Carrot sticks

Directions:

Cook pasta as per instructions given on your package.

To make the balls, take a small bowl and prepare a mixture of vinegar, butter, sauce, and salt. Now mix it well. Separate ¼ cup of this mixture and set it aside. Add chicken mince and make small balls with this mixture. Now take the marinade in a large bowl and add chicken balls in this mixture. Mix the balls and keep in the refrigerator for 60 minutes.

Dressing:

Take a small bowl mix cheese, mayonnaise, salt, and sour cream. Mix it well and keep in refrigerator until you serve it.

Now keep an oven rack in the broiler with 8" height. Now preheat a broiler and cover the baking sheet with foil. Keep the balls in a row on the baking sheet with consistent space. Let it broil for 14 to 16 minutes and turn once. Keep this procedure continue until you make the balls crispy. Keep an eye on the balls to avoid burning.

Now transfer pasta on the serving plate, put meatballs on pasta and spread the hot sauce mixture on the top and serve with dressing and carrot sticks.

Recipe 19: Avocado Pasta with Chicken

Cooking Time: 10 minutes

Servings: 6

Ingredients:

- 1 chopped poblano pepper
- Pasta: 8 oz.
- 1 chopped tomato

- 1 lime

- ¼ teaspoon sea salt

- ½ chopped onion

- Chicken (cooked and cubed): 2 cups

- 3 tablespoons chopped cilantro

- ¼ teaspoon cayenne pepper

- 4 avocados, halved (pitted)

Directions:

Cook pasta as per instructions given on the package.

Take a medium bowl and mix pepper, tomato, onion, cilantro, chicken and salt. Take one spoon of the mixture and keep it in the avocado half. You can scoop out some pulp to use in the salsa. Spread pasta in a plate and top it with avocado. Sprinkle lime juice on it and serve. You can use tuna in salsa as well.

Recipe 20: BBQ Turkey Pasta

Cooking Time: 30 minutes

Servings: 4

Ingredients:

- 1 pound raw turkey breast

- ½ teaspoon cayenne pepper

- ½ chopped bell pepper

- ½ chopped onion

- Pasta: 8 oz.

- ½ chopped red pepper

- 1 cup barbecue sauce

- 4-grain hamburger rolls, sliced

Directions:

Cook pasta as per instructions given on the package.

Great a nonstick cooking pan with cooking oil and add the turkey to let it brown. It may take almost 10 minutes. Remove any liquid and add onion and peppers to cook almost 3 minutes. Add cayenne pepper and barbecue sauces and cook for almost 2 minutes. Take one-half of the half and top with turkey mixture and cover with another half of the bun. Serve with pasta and a low fat and low sugar sauce.

Chapter 5 – Pasta Dessert Recipe

If you want to enjoy sweet desserts, there are a few recipes for you. These are extremely delicious and healthy:

Recipe 21: Vermicelli Pudding

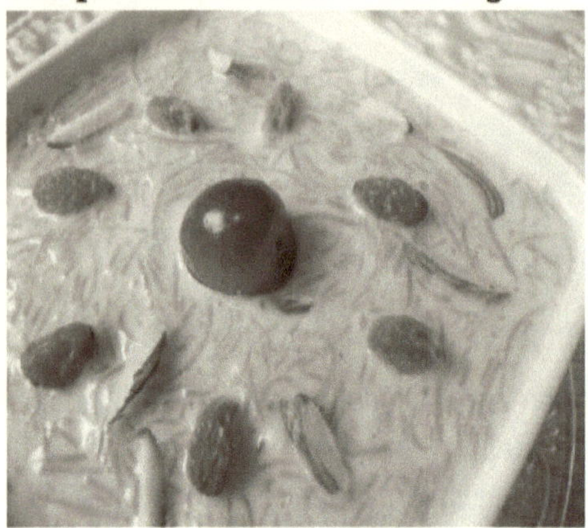

Cooking Time: 40 minutes

Servings: 4

Ingredients:

- Milk: 1-quart
- White sugar: 5 tablespoons
- Vermicelli pasta (broken): 8 ounce
- Raisins: 8
- Cardamom seeds: 8

Directions:

Pour milk in one saucepan and add cardamom seeds and sugar. Let them boil on medium heat and reduce heat to simmer for almost 5 minutes. Mix raisins and broken pasta into milk and let them cook for almost 5 minutes to let the cream thick. Turn off heat and leave this mixture for almost 15 minutes. If the pudding is thick, you can add little milk. Serve hot.

Recipe 22: Spaghetti Pudding

Cooking Time: 55 minutes

Servings: 4

Ingredients:

- Butter: 2 tablespoons
- Milk: 2 cups
- Chopped cashews: 2 tablespoons
- Uncooked pasta: 4 ounces
- White sugar: 6 tablespoons
- Raisins: 2 tablespoons

Directions:

Take a large cooking pan and put it on medium heat to melt butter. Fry raisins and cashews to turn them golden brown. Remove these ingredients from pan and keep it aside. Fry pasta (dry) pieces in the pan to let them golden brown for almost 5 minutes.

Add milk to this pan and increase heat. Let the milk boil and reduce heat to low. Simmer until the spaghetti turns soft and the milk turns thick. Mix cashews, raisins and sugar. Take off from heat and leave for 30 minutes. Serve cold or hot.

Recipe 23: Pasta Fruit Salad

Cooking Time: 1 hours 15 minutes

Servings: 7

Ingredients:

- Macaroni: 12 ounces
- Vanilla pudding mix: 3.5 ounce
- Milk: 1 ½ cups
- Mandarin oranges (drained): 11 ounces
- Crushed pineapple: 20 ounce
- Fruit cocktail (drained): 15.25 ounce
- Maraschino cherries (drained): 10 ounces
- Whipped topping: 8 ounces

Directions:

Take salted water in a pot and let it boil. Cook pasta according to the instructions given on the package and rinse under water.

Follow the directions of pudding to prepare it, but use only 1.5 cups milk and keep in refrigerator to chill.

Take a large bowl and mix pudding and pasta. Mix these ingredients well and add fruit cocktail, pineapples, oranges and cherries. Mix whipped cream and serve chilled.

Recipe 24: Sweet Pasta

Cooking Time: 15 minutes

Servings: 8

Ingredients:

- Half-and-half: 1 pint
- Lemon zest: 1 lemon
- Orange zest: 1 orange
- Honey: 2 tablespoons
- Kosher salt: 1 pinch
- Linguine: 12 ounces
- Lemon juice: 1 tablespoon
- Semisweet chocolate: 3 ounces
- Hazelnuts (chopped): 1/4 cup

Directions:

Take one large pot filled with salted water and boil water on high heat.

Take a heavy skillet and pour cream to heat it. Add salt, zest and honey to cook on medium heat. Be careful because the cream shouldn't boil so mix occasionally for almost 4 minutes.

In the meantime, add pasta to boiling water and cook until tender. Mix occasionally for almost 2 to 3 minutes. Drain pasta and put it in the heavy skillet with cream. Add lemon juice and mix well.

Take serving dishes and transfer pasta to dishes. Garnish with chocolate and hazelnuts. Serve.

Recipe 25: Fried Pasta Dessert

Cooking Time: 30 minutes

Servings: 2 to 3

Cooking Time: 30 minutes

Servings: 2 to 3

Ingredients:

- Angel-hair pasta: 1/3 pound
- Vanilla beans: 2
- Crème Fraiche: 1 cup
- Honey divided: 4 tablespoons
- Orange zest: 1 teaspoon
- Lemon zest: 1 teaspoon
- One pinches cinnamon
- Vegetable oil, for frying
- Toasted walnuts: 2 tablespoons

Directions:

Cook pasta as per instructions that are given on the package, drain and keep it aside.

Take a bowl, whisk vanilla seeds, cream and honey (1 tablespoon). Mix them well and set aside.

Take another bowl and whisk remaining honey, lemon zest, and orange zest along with cinnamon. Keep this bowl aside.

Take a deep pan, heat oil on high flame and once the temperature reaches 375 degrees F, fry cooked pasta in twirled haystacks. Flip every haystack halfway until it becomes golden and crispy. In the absence of a thermometer, you can put one pinch cornstarch to your pan because it will fry immediately as your oil is ready to cook pasta.

Set pasta on a plate, drizzle honey mixture and cream sauce. Garnish with walnuts and serve.

Conclusion

recipes of the pasta diet because the unique combination of ingredients will keep you full and reduce your craving. The fresh fruits and vegetables are high in fiber and more filling. You can't consume starchy vegetables because they are greater in calories. Pasta has specific options of power foods, such as considering ten types of canned soups and select one with less salt and sugar. You need more fiber and healthy fat in your regular diet. They offer hundreds of recipes with their particular points that you can eat during your diet. If your prepared dish is not available in their provided database, then you can calculate calories of a particular dish on a free tool.

Include Proteins in Your Regular Diet

Protein should be an important part of your diet to get rid of stubborn belly fat. You can follow a diet for almost two months with 30% protein, 40% carbs, and 30% healthy fat. It will prove helpful to get rid of additional belly fat. Including protein in your diet will be a long term strategy for you to lose weight.

Avoid Sugar and Sugar Beverages

You need to avoid liquid sugar because it is worse for you as your brain can't acknowledge the liquid sugar in the same way as solid calories. If you drink the more sugar-sweetened drink, then you will end up eating more calories.

Cut Carbohydrates from Your Diet

If you want to reduce belly fat, then you should cut carbohydrates from your regular diet. By decreasing carbs, your hunger will go down, and you may lose weight. You need to follow a low-carb and low-fat diet to target your belly fat. Avoid white bread, rice, and pasta and keep your protein intake high. If you want to lose weight fast, then it is important to cut down your carb intake up to 50 grams per day.

Eat Fiber Rich Food

Try to include green leafy vegetables and fresh fruits in your regular diet. It will help you to get rid of belly fat. Fresh fruits and vegetables will prove helpful, and you should take almost 14 grams of fiber on a regular basis for a

10% decrease in the calorie intake. It helps you have a flat belly and reduce harmful belly fat.

Make a Food Journal

It is important to keep a record of how much you are eating because excessive consumption of fiber and protein will be harmful to you. If you want to boost the 25 to 30% protein intake, then you have to write it in a food journal to calculate the total calories you need to consume in a day.

Do ' s and Don ' ts of Healthy Diet

- You can load your regular meals with fruits and vegetable-carrying low calories because these are higher in fiber and can easily satisfy your craving.

- Stick to your calorie target because these are assigned to you by protein, carb, calories, fiber and fat requirements of your body. It is also based on the fact that how hard your body can do the workout to burn off the fat. You can check calories with your smartphone or web.

- Alcohol is not good to overdo them. Use it in moderation because 12-ounce beers often low-calories. If you spend all the points in the alcohol intake, then what will you do for the rest of the day.